In · Time · of · Need

Storms

by Sean Connolly

Smart Apple Media

Published by Smart Apple Media
2140 Howard Drive West
North Mankato, Minnesota 56003

Design by Ian Butterworth

Photographs by:
Corbis (AFP, Bettmann, Bohemian Nomad Picturemakers,
Gary Braasch, CORBIS SYGMA, Jeff Curtes, Robert Dowling,
Najlah Feanny, Al Francekevich, Michael Freeman, S.P. Gillette,
Chris Golley, Gunter Marx Photography, Jose Luis Pelaez, Inc.,
Chuck Keeler, Jr., Matthias Kulka, Jim McDonald, Reuters,
Royalty-Free, Ariel Skelley, Ray Soto, Steve Starr, Stocktrek,
SCOTT TAKUSHI/CORBIS SYGMA, TUTTLE/WICHITA
EAGLE BEACON/CORBIS SYGMA, A & J Verkaik)

Library of Congress Cataloging-in-Publication Data

Connolly, Sean, 1956–
Storms / by Sean Connolly.
p. cm. — (In time of need)
Includes index.
Summary: Describes various types of storms, giving specific
examples of them in history.
ISBN 1-58340-393-0
1. Storms—Juvenile literature. [1. Storms.] I. Title.

QC941.3.C66 2004
363.34'92—dc21
2003050392

First Edition

2 4 6 8 9 7 5 3 1

Contents

Restless
Weather

Everyone is interested in the weather. We depend on clear weather for picnics and outdoor sports events, while farmers need regular rainfall to make sure their crops grow. In most parts of the world, people experience changes in weather: it may be sunny or cloudy, with wind, rain, or snow. Bad weather might be a cause for disappointment—or perhaps relief, when rain is needed for crops—but it does not usually cause damage.

But sometimes bad weather can become severe and cause enormous amounts of damage—or even death. Storms and other types of extreme weather can destroy houses, level towns, and ravage large areas of a country. Hundreds of years ago, these storms caused even more damage because people did not expect them. Nowadays, **meteorologists** predict many of the worst storms days in advance. This information can save lives and protect property—but it cannot change the weather. Even with the best planning, people are powerless to stop the storm from tearing their houses apart.

Above: The temperature of lightning is estimated to be about 50,000 °F (27,760 °C)—hotter than the surface of the sun. Left: Clear, sunny days are perfect for a picnic at the beach.

Constant Change

The weather on our planet is constantly changing. Even when it seems the same for days on end, there are changes taking place in the **atmosphere** high above us. As the sun heats air and water, the warm air and **evaporated** water rise. The **air pressure** drops in places where heated air is rising. More air rushes in to fill the space it leaves behind. This air rushing in is called wind. Warm air eventually cools down and sinks. Because Earth spins, the air curves or spirals as it descends, and it comes down in a different place from where it began.

Different parts of Earth warm up faster than others, and the air in different places warms up at different rates. These differences affect the weather by pushing more or less air upward, releasing more or less water in the sky, and producing more or less wind down below. Air rising slowly releases its water to produce clouds, which are floating masses of tiny water particles and ice crystals. Stronger movement upward draws up more water than can stay in the clouds. The extra water falls back to the ground as rain. Rain can fall steadily and gently or more violently—as in a storm.

It takes about one million cloud droplets to provide enough water for one raindrop.

5

Types of Storms

The main ingredients of most storms are rain and wind. Nearly every storm, great or small, constantly draws up and relases air and water as it spins. Some of the largest storms, called **hurricanes**, develop over warm oceans by sucking up and then releasing huge amounts of rain. The power of the warming air also produces the strong winds of a hurricane.

Severe thunderstorms can create the most destructive storms on the planet: tornadoes. Although they usually last only a few minutes and affect a very small area, tornadoes can suck up nearly anything in their path.

Winter storms in cold places also draw water up from oceans and lakes, but the colder air temperature means that the water falls as snow or ice. Drifting snow, blown by strong winds, is created by **blizzards** and other winter snowstorms.

At any given time, there are nearly 2,000 thunderstorm cells over the planet. The United States has more than 100,000 thunderstorms annually, while the global average is 16 million!

SHAPING HISTORY

Powerful storms have sometimes played a part in world history. One of the earliest stories, in the Bible, tells of 40 days of rain that created a flood and destroyed most of the world. Sometimes people are saved by storms. In 1281, Chinese Emperor Kublai Khan sent a force of 140,000 soldiers across the sea to invade Japan. As they approached Japan, a terrible typhoon sank many of the warships and killed about half of the soldiers. England was similarly saved in 1588. King Philip of Spain sent an armada of 130 ships to attack England. Strong winds in the English Channel sank many of them, along with 28,000 Spanish soldiers.

Above: An illustration depicting the Spanish Armada.

Swirling Winds

Some of the largest and most powerful storms are hurricanes, which develop over the warm ocean water near the **equator**. The word "hurricane" comes from the language of the Taino people, Native Americans who lived on the islands of the Caribbean Sea, where hurricanes are common. It means "windy storm." The western Pacific Ocean is another area that is frequently hit by hurricanes. People there refer to them as **typhoons**, from Chinese words meaning "great wind."

Above: From space, the eye of a hurricane and its menacing spiral shape are clearly visible.
Left: When funnel clouds touch down, the swirling winds can wreak terrible destruction.

Tropical Trouble

The waters of **tropical** regions are always warm, but in the late summer they are at their warmest. This warm, damp air can easily be sucked or forced upward to form a storm. With a constant source of warm air and water, the storm may continue to grow. The air pressure drops lower and lower, sucking in air from outside at greater and greater speeds and building up in a swirling shape.

Weather experts use the term "tropical storm" to describe a storm with a steady wind speed of between 39 and 73 miles (63–117 km) per hour. A tropical storm officially becomes a hurricane when winds reach 74 miles (119 km) or more per hour, over an area 150 miles (240 km) or more wide. Hurricane winds are strongest near the center, or **eye**, of the storm, which looks like the hole of a giant spinning donut when seen from above. In the eye, the winds are calmer, and there are no clouds. The strength of a hurricane is rated from one to five. The mildest, category one, has winds of at least 74 miles (119 km) per hour. The strongest, category five, has winds blowing more than 155 miles (250 km) per hour.

Below: Heavy rain and dangerous winds battered the coast of Guadeloupe as Cyclone Luis struck the area in September 1995.

TROPICAL STORMS

Severe damage and flooding can also be caused by tropical storms that do not become strong enough to be called hurricanes. Tropical storm Alberto made landfall near Destin, Florida, on July 3, 1994, causing little damage. But Alberto's destruction was just beginning. For four days, the storm drifted over eastern Alabama and western Georgia, dumping heavy rains and causing widespread flooding. A record-breaking 21 inches (53 cm) of rain fell in a 24-hour period in Americus, Georgia. Alberto's heavy rains and floods caused more than $500 million of property damage. Twenty-eight people in Georgia and two in Alabama lost their lives.

Hitting Land

Many hurricanes die down at sea, well away from land. If they make **landfall**, they may destroy buildings, knock down trees and electrical wires, and cause severe flooding. In October 1998, Hurricane Mitch slammed into Central America, leaving very little standing. The countries hardest hit were Honduras, Guatemala, El Salvador, and Nicaragua. Massive **landslides**, floods, and strong winds killed more than 6,000 people and left more than 150,000 people homeless in Honduras alone.

Without a fresh supply of water, hurricanes run out of power about a day after making landfall. Some hurricanes, however, make landfall briefly and then turn back to sea to gather more power. They can travel up the east coast of the United States, well away from typical hurricane "hot spots." On the afternoon of September 21, 1938, a terrible hurricane struck Long Island and southern New England, killing nearly 700 people, knocking down 275 million trees, thousands of buildings, and nearly 20,000 miles (32,180 km) of power and telephone lines. Several major cities, including parts of New York and Boston, were severely flooded.

Above: A Florida resident returns to his home to look for salvageable items after Hurricane Andrew in 1992. Left: Torrential rain and flooding can cause roadways to erode and crumble.

HURRICANE NAMES

During the course of a storm season, many tropical storms can develop, and several of them grow into hurricanes. At times, there are multiple hurricanes threatening the same part of the world. Weather experts give the storms names so that people can keep track of them in weather reports. Each area of the world has its own list of names, which is drawn up before the storm season begins. The names are given in alphabetical order (skipping Q, U, X, Y, and Z) and the list switches between girls' names and boys' names. The names for the 2003 hurricane season in eastern North America were Ana, Bill, Claudette, Danny, Erika, Fabian, Grace, Henri, Isabel, Juan, Kate, Larry, Mindy, Nicholas, Odette, Peter, Rose, Sam, Teresa, Victor, and Wanda.

Left: In 1998, Hurricane Mitch caused widespread flooding and massive landslides throughout Central America. This boy's neighborhood was almost entirely destroyed when a hillside overlooking his village gave way.

TORNADO ALLEY

Many of the 800 or so tornadoes that develop each year in the United States occur in an area nicknamed "Tornado Alley." This area lies between the Mississippi River and the Rocky Mountains. In spring and early summer, moist, warm air moves up from the Gulf of Mexico and hits colder air moving down from Canada. The two air masses clash to produce violent storms. Tornadoes are created by the strongest of these thunderstorms.

Twister!

The most powerful storms on Earth are tornadoes. Luckily, a tornado lasts only a short while—usually only minutes—and affects a small area. But with winds swirling at speeds of up to 300 miles (480 km) per hour, a tornado destroys nearly everything in its path. It can cause great tragedy in a brief period of time. A tornado that swept through parts of Missouri, Indiana, and Illinois on March 18, 1925, killed 689 people.

A tornado is a rapidly spinning funnel of air that extends down from a thundercloud to the ground. Some people call tornadoes "twisters" because of this spinning movement. Weather experts know what sort of conditions produce a tornado, but they can never be sure exactly where or when a tornado will strike.

When the funnel touches the ground, it sucks up everything in its way, tearing things apart or flinging them far away. The funnel looks dark because of all the dust it has sucked up. Tornadoes that touch down on water are called **waterspouts**. Waterspouts can suck up water, fish, and even boats.

Above: When tornadoes touch down in cities or populated areas, the results can be deadly.
Left: The same warm, moist air that creates hurricanes in tropical regions can create severe thunderstorms that cause tornadoes farther inland.

"The air was filled with 10,000 things. Boards, poles, cans . . . stoves, whole sides of the little frame houses, in some cases the houses themselves, were picked up and smashed to earth. And living beings, too. A baby was blown from its mother's arms. A cow, picked up by the wind, was hurled into the village restaurant."

An account in the St. Louis Post-Dispatch *of a deadly tornado on March 20, 1925*

"The appearance of the water rising in the air was perfectly white, like a heavy spray or stream. It spread out as it rose, and in a very short time, perhaps half a minute, the cloud reached and enveloped it, and all was black to the surface of the water."

Dr. O. F. Thomas's description of a waterspout in New Richmond, Wisconsin, on June 12, 1899

Left: Just like tornadoes on land, waterspouts on the open sea have powerful winds. Large waterspouts can suck fish and boats right out of the water.

Snow and Blizzards

Rain forms as snow high up in the cold clouds. If the temperature on the ground is above freezing, it melts and becomes rain as it falls. If the temperature on the ground is cold enough, the snow never melts on its way down, but floats to Earth as snow. Sometimes, the snow falls in a severe storm, with strong winds blowing it into drifts and making it hard to see. Some parts of the United States have blizzards in the winter and tornadoes in the summer, but most places that are hit by severe snowstorms rarely have hurricanes (which affect warmer areas).

Left: When a fast-moving blizzard dumped more than two feet (60 cm) of snow in Buffalo, New York, drivers were forced to abandon their vehicles in the wintry gridlock.

Right: Blizzards and ice storms create perilous driving conditions. This car overturned in the snow after sliding off a slick highway in Canada.

Severe snowstorms and blizzards can cause terrible damage. Cars and trucks often crash because of slippery roads, and the heavy snow can cause power lines and even trees to come toppling down. With power lines down, many homes lose their heat, and the freezing temperatures pose another danger.

WHAT IS A BLIZZARD?

People often use the word "blizzard" to describe any mix of wind and snow. But it is important to know what weather experts mean when they predict a blizzard, because it is one of the most frightening of all storms. Blizzards usually have temperatures below 20 °F (-7 °C) and wind speeds of 35 miles (55 km) or more per hour. The combination of snow and wind reduces VISIBILITY to one-quarter mile (400 m) or less for at least three hours. A severe blizzard has temperatures near or below 10 °F (-12 °C), winds of at least 45 miles (75 km) per hour, and visibility reduced to near zero.

THE STORM OF THE CENTURY

On March 12 and 13, 1993, the eastern half of the United States was hit by a blizzard that became known as the "Storm of the Century," or the "Superstorm." It was terribly damaging, killing more than 270 people and causing as much as $6 billion in damage. The storm came late in the winter, catching many people by surprise. But this terrible blizzard also struck many areas that do not normally see much snow. About 17 inches (43 cm) fell on Birmingham, Alabama, and 56 inches (142 cm) covered Mount LeConte, Tennessee.

No one really knows where the snowiest place on Earth is, but the biggest snowfalls are often recorded in the U.S. The Rocky Mountains have an average snowfall of between 300 and 400 inches (7.5–10.25 m). Paradise Ranger Station in the Rockies once recorded 1,224 inches (30 m) of snow in a single year.

At the Scene

Powerful storms strike quickly. An area that has been hit can easily become cut off by fallen buildings and trees, rising floodwaters, or drifting snow. Even after the damaging winds have died down, heavy rain and snow can keep roads and train lines blocked. Weather conditions might also make it difficult—if not impossible—for rescue aircraft to arrive.

The first people who can help are those who are in the area already. Some emergency services, such as the coast guard and **paramedics**, might be on hand to help local police and fire services. Often these services rely on other local people who are prepared to lend a hand.

Above: Storm-damaged trees can sometimes block the way for emergency help.
Left: When floodwaters engulfed Grand Forks, North Dakota, members of the Coast Guard used a motor boat to inspect the town streets.

Keeping People Calm

People who have gone without food and sleep—and who might not know whether their houses are still standing—sometimes panic. George Metts is a paramedic who was assigned to a storm shelter in the local high school in McClellanville, South Carolina, on September 21, 1989. McClellanville was at the heart of the coastal stretch pounded by Hurricane Hugo. Floodwaters were rising, even inside the high school. Metts gathered a group of about a dozen people onto a stage: "We were totally trapped. The **tidal surge** had risen so rapidly that we had no time to call for help. My walkie-talkie had gotten wet earlier, and now it had fallen into the inky darkness. We were on our own. The water was still rising, and those that could were packed like sardines on the stage."

This all became too much for one woman, who began breathing very quickly (a sign of panic). Metts knew that this panic could easily spread to the others, and people might be knocked into the dark waters all around them if things got out of hand. Luckily, Metts was able to calm the woman. The water reached its peak below the stage, and the group was rescued several hours later.

Left: When floodwaters make roads impassable, rescue workers often use helicopters to reach victims and take them to safety.

Combining Forces

A **cyclone** known simply as "2A" hit Pakistan's southeastern coast on May 20, 1999. The storm took many people by surprise because it had been heading for neighboring India and changed course at the last minute. Many coastal fishing villages were badly damaged. High winds and huge waves destroyed many of the houses, which were made of mud. Wind and flood damage blocked many land routes to the storm area, so the Pakistani navy took the lead in sending emergency relief teams. This quick action saved many lives by helping to get doctors and medical equipment to the worst-affected areas. Emergency workers from the Pakistani army were able to join these relief teams once floodwaters went down and roads were opened again.

Above: Relief trucks cross a flooded road after a powerful cyclone struck Pakistan and India in 1999.

DOUBLE TROUBLE

Southeast Africa was hit by two cyclones just a week apart in March and April 2000. The first, Cyclone Eline, knocked down trees and poured down rain. Rivers began to swell and burst their banks, especially on the low-lying coastal plains of Mozambique. The second cyclone, called Gloria, also hit Mozambique hardest and added coastal floods to the country's problems. Neighboring countries such as South Africa sent planes and helicopters to search for more than 100,000 people who were missing. Zambia and Lesotho—two of the poorest countries in Africa—sent their only cargo planes to deliver food and medicine to Mozambique. The United Nations Children's Fund (UNICEF), the International Red Cross, and many other countries realized how severe the problem was. But they needed to tell the world to act quickly. "If the governments of the world are going to help, the time is now—not tomorrow or the next day," stated UNICEF chief Carol Bellamy.

Left: In 1998, a U.S. Army helicopter unloads food and water for victims of Hurricane Mitch in Honduras.

Reaching Out

We have all seen disasters on television. Hurricanes and tornadoes leave a trail of destruction behind them. It is often hard to decide where to start rebuilding. Wealthy countries such as the United States and Japan regularly face such disasters. Their governments assess the scene of destruction and decide whether it requires government help. A badly hit area may be declared a "disaster area." This means that government money can be used for rescues, repairs, and rebuilding.

Many other countries are less well off. A natural disaster, such as a destructive storm, can affect the country for years. When there is little money available from their own governments, disaster survivors in such countries often look to the wider world for help.

Above: Workers pour sand to reconstruct a beach in Cancun, Mexico, after a hurricane.
Left: Downtown Grand Forks, North Dakota, was declared a disaster area after the floodwaters of the Red River engulfed the city in the spring of 1997.

Helping Hands

There are many organizations that offer help in emergencies. Many of these organizations are supported by the United Nations (U.N.), a cooperative body that includes nearly every country in the world. In addition to a range of emergency relief groups that provide immediate help after a disaster, the U.N. has organizations that can offer help with a country's long-term recovery in areas such as healthcare, education, and food supply.

There are many other international organizations that are prepared to respond to a disaster. International Rescue Corps has volunteers that help pull people from wrecked buildings and other dangerous places. The International Federation of the Red Cross and Red Crescent Societies has been offering medical and food aid in emergencies for nearly 150 years. CARE (Cooperative for American Relief Everywhere) International and many religious organizations concentrate on making sure that people have shelter and enough to eat.

Below: Victims often rely on government and international aid organizations to deliver food and supplies after storm disasters strike.

PACIFIC MIRACLE

As the year 2002 drew to an end, a terrible cyclone named Zoe swept across the Solomon Islands in the South Pacific. With winds of up to 200 miles (320 km) per hour, Zoe was one of the worst storms ever seen in the region. Waves crashed into the islands, sweeping away villages and flattening trees. Radio contact with some of the smaller islands was cut off during the storm, and there was no sign of human life when planes flew overhead several days later. The planes could not land because the islands had no landing fields.

Exactly a week after the cyclone struck, a New Zealand cameraman named Geoff Mackley landed on the island of Tikopia by helicopter. To his surprise, he was greeted by many of the more than 1,000 people who live on Tikopia. They told him that they had taken shelter in mountain caves as soon as the storm hit.

Top and bottom right: Sand and palm tree stumps are all that remain of two remote villages on the island of Tikopia, after Hurricane Zoe devastated the Solomon Islands in 2002.

Wider Problems

Sometimes destructive storms affect areas that are still trying to pick up the pieces after an earlier disaster. That was the case in southern Africa in March and April 2000. A severe **drought**, lasting several growing seasons, had already ruined crops and left people weak and hungry. Then two powerful cyclones slammed into the coast, dumping heavy rains and creating terrible floods.

The governments of the worst-affected countries (Mozambique, South Africa, Zimbabwe, and Botswana) met with international relief and aid groups. They needed to work out a plan that would save people immediately after the cyclones. But they also had to think ahead, so that the local people would eventually be able to work and support themselves. The U.N. World Food Program took the lead in this second job. It launched a $6.8 million emergency aid operation to help southern African farmers rebuild their homes and prepare for another harvest.

"That day it rained in torrents. I thought we were all lost, but we only lost things that can be replaced."
Daysi Martinez, recalling conditions during Hurricane Mitch before aid from World Vision arrived in El Salvador

"I thought I would see hundreds of dead bodies, but instead we were just overwhelmed with people running toward us."
Photographer Geoff Mackley after landing on Tikopia in January 2003, a week after Cyclone Zoe hit the island

"The waves were 12 feet high and the seawater was pouring into our homes. Nearly everything we had was destroyed."
Fisherman Arif Suleman, describing the cyclone that hit Dwarka, Pakistan, on May 20, 1999

"CARE International was a **godsend**. If it had not been for them, thousands of people around Paradip would have starved."
An eyewitness remembers the days after a cyclone swept through the Indian city of Paradip in November 1999

Left: Severe storms can often lead to greater problems. When Hurricane Mitch struck Honduras in 1998, it caused the Choluteca River to burst its banks—resulting in devastating flood damage.

Building
Again

On September 22, 1938, people living by Misquamicut Beach, Rhode Island, returned to their neighborhood after a powerful hurricane pounded the New England coastline. Most had spent the night in schools and other emergency centers in nearby Westerly and Charlestown. They found a scene of almost total destruction. Of about 500 houses in one neighborhood, only five escaped damage. For most people it was time to think of repairs. For others, the job looked bigger—they would have to rebuild from scratch.

Above: People working to rebuild a bridge (left) in Honduras that was destroyed by Hurricane Mitch in 1998. After severe storms, residents must work together to repair and rebuild their communities.

A Familiar Story

The Rhode Islanders were not alone on that day in 1938. Hundreds of thousands of people in New England and New York faced similar problems. And each year, across the world, dozens of storms create similar destruction. People must find out how—and if—they can afford to repair or replace their damaged property.

Many people living in the United States, Canada, and Europe have **insurance** on their houses. They pay a certain amount each year to insurance companies. If a disaster causes damage to the house, the insurance company pays for repairs. Most people around the world do not have insurance. They lose everything if a hurricane or tornado knocks down their house. If they are lucky, their government or a relief organization will help them rebuild or find a new place to live.

Below: When homes are destroyed by storms, many people rely on insurance money to help rebuild.

DIRTY TRICKS

Sometimes a disaster can lead to other unexpected troubles for the people who were affected. Andrew, a powerful hurricane, caused great damage around Miami, Florida, in 1992. Thousands of homes were destroyed, and thousands of residents contacted their insurance companies. Unfortunately, the insurance inspectors, who assess what repairs are needed, were overloaded by calls. Many people had to wait months just to find out what their insurance company would pay for. Even when repair work was underway, the residents faced problems. There was too much work for local carpenters and builders to handle, and many unreliable people pretended to be builders. They did a bad job and used poor materials, so some of the people found their houses no better off—and their insurance money gone.

On the Alert

We can do nothing to stop the weather. That is especially true of storms, which most people would love to prevent. But just as someone might pack a raincoat and an umbrella when the weather turns cloudy, towns, cities, and even countries can make sure that they are prepared.

One way of being prepared is to use the most advanced tools and scientific methods to keep track of the weather. But good scientists never ignore the experience passed down from earlier times. There is real scientific truth behind such sayings as "Red sky at night, sailor's delight: red sky at morning, sailor take warning." Old stories,

Above: A meteorologist tracks a hurricane by studying satellite information.
Left: Meteorologists across the world rely on satellite images to track storms.

passed down by word of mouth, tell us about birdsongs, the color of daylight, and other natural things that change just before a hurricane or tornado hits.

Another important part of being prepared is to pass the news of an approaching storm on to the public. Giving people a clear idea of what is coming—and the danger they face if they remain in the path of a major storm—can save many lives. The U.S. National Weather Service does just that, along with other organizations such as the National Hurricane Center.

Below: Satellite images such as this help predict dangerous weather, giving people time to prepare for storms.

wwwghcc.msfc.nasa.gov

3 Mar 2001
04:01 UTC

No Clouds
Warm Surface Temps

Weak Clouds
Low Altitudes

Intense Cl
High Altite

LEARNING FROM A TRAGEDY

Most countries that regularly have hurricanes make sure that the public is warned about approaching storms in time to prepare or EVACUATE. In the U.S., weather warnings became much stricter after a tragedy that took place in 1969. That year, Hurricane Camille created a coastal flood that was a record 24.5 feet (7.5 m) above sea level at Pass Christian, Mississippi. Twenty-five residents of an apartment complex refused to leave. Instead, they threw a "hurricane party" in Camille's honor. Camille's raging flood destroyed the complex, and only two people survived the storm. Since that tragedy, local police and emergency forces try to make sure that people understand and obey severe weather warnings.

STORMREADY

One of the best ways of being prepared for a severe storm is to make sure that everyone knows exactly how storms do their damage and what to do when they hit. The U.S. National Weather Service has a nationwide program, known as StormReady, to offer advice. StormReady helps towns and cities develop plans to handle all types of severe weather—from tornadoes to TSUNAMIS. To be officially StormReady, a community must:

• establish a 24-hour warning point (a place where people can see storm alerts) and emergency operations center;

• create a system that keeps track of local weather conditions;

• have more than one way to receive severe weather warnings and forecasts and to alert the public (so that if one communications system is knocked out by the storm, there is a backup system);

• make presentations and have meetings to convince people to be ready at all times; and

• develop an emergency weather plan that includes training severe weather spotters and practicing for a weather emergency.

"Men are slow to believe they might be the unwilling victims of like disasters."
A comment in the local newspaper after a terrible tornado hit New Richmond, Wisconsin, in June 1899

Below: With the aid of weather forecasts and warnings, people can avoid getting trapped in dangerous situations, such as sailing during a storm.

Below: A satellite photo of a hurricane.

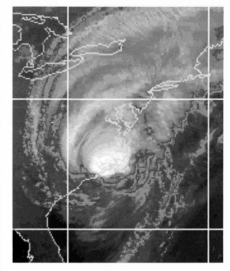

WEATHER WARNINGS

The U.S. National Hurricane Center makes people aware of dangerous storms that it is tracking. It regularly cuts into local television and radio programs to tell people when and where a storm is likely to hit. The U.S. National Weather Service, like national weather organizations in other countries, makes similar warnings for tornadoes, blizzards, and other severe weather. Below are some of the terms used in warnings about hurricanes.

• HURRICANE WATCH Threat of hurricane conditions within 24 to 36 hours.

• HURRICANE WARNING Hurricane conditions are expected to strike an area in 24 hours or less. Hurricane conditions include winds of 74 miles (119 km) or more per hour and dangerously high tides and waves. People should begin protecting life and property as soon as the warning is given.

• FLASH FLOOD WATCH Stay alert for flash floods.

• FLASH FLOOD WARNING A flash flood is likely to hit very soon; take immediate action.

Glossary

air pressure the measure of how heavily air is pressing down

assessing examining carefully in order to assign a value or other judgment

atmosphere the layers of gases surrounding Earth

blizzards severe snowstorms with high winds

cyclone another word for a hurricane

drought a long period with no rain

equator an imaginary line around Earth that is halfway between the North and South poles

evacuate to escape from a dangerous place

evaporated (for a liquid) changed into a gas by heat and dispersed into the air

eye the calm center of a hurricane

godsend an unexpected bit of good luck or kindness

hurricanes powerful storms developing over the ocean and having winds of 74 miles (119 km) or more per hour

insurance protection against loss or damage

landfall the place where a storm reaches the coast

landslides large amounts of earth or mud that come loose and slip down a hill or mountainside

meteorologists scientists who study the weather

paramedics people trained to give medical help at the scene of an accident or disaster

tidal surge a flood caused when strong winds blow high tide waters inland

tropical having to do with the warmest parts of Earth, near the equator

tsunamis huge waves caused by earthquakes or underwater volcanoes

typhoons hurricanes

visibility the maximum distance at which an object can be seen

waterspouts funnels of water created when a tornado touches a lake or the sea

Further Information

Books

Branley, Franklyn M. *Flash, Crash, Rumble, and Roll.* New York: HarperCollins Juvenile Books, 1999.

Burroughs, William James (ed.). *Weather: Nature Company Guides.* New York: Time Life, 1996.

Dewitt, Lynda. *What Will the Weather Be?* New York: HarperTrophy, 1993.

Osborne, Will, and Osborne, Mary Pope. *Twisters and Other Terrible Storms.* New York: Random House, 2003.

Web sites

Storm Spotter's Guide
http://www.srh.noaa.gov/oun/skywarn/spotterguide.html

Stormy Weather
http://www.educationcentral.org/stormy

What Forces Affect Our Weather?
http://www.learner.org/exhibits/weather

Index